J.K. ROWLING

REVISED EDITION

Colleen Sexton

Twenty-First Century Books
Minneapolis

For my parents, Jim and Nancy Sexton, who introduced me to the magic of books. And in memory of my uncle, Bob Hughes, who delighted in the adventures of Harry Potter.

Twenty-First Century Books
A division of Lerner Publishing Group, Inc.
241 First Avenue North
Minneapolis, MN 55401 U.S.A.

Website addresses: www.lernerbooks.com
www.biography.com

Library of Congress Cataloging-in-Publication Data

Sexton, Colleen A., 1967–
    J.K. Rowling / by Colleen A. Sexton. — Rev. ed.
        p.   cm. — (Biography)
    Includes bibliographical references (p.   ) and index.
    ISBN 978–0–8225–7949–6 (lib. bdg. : alk. paper)
    1. Rowling, J. K.—Juvenile literature. 2. Authors, English—20th century—Biography—Juvenile literature. 3. Potter, Harry (Fictitious character)—Juvenile literature. 4. Children's stories—Authorship—Juvenile literature. I. Title.
    PR6068.O93Z8553 2008
    823'.914—dc22
    [B]   2007000219

Manufactured in the United States of America
1 2 3 4 5 6 – BP – 13 12 11 10 09 08

CONTENTS

J. K. Rowling waves to the crowd before beginning to read from
one of her Harry Potter books at the SkyDome in Toronto, Canada.

INTRODUCTION

On an autumn day in 2000, a rowdy crowd of twenty thousand people poured into the SkyDome in Toronto, Canada. They were there for a big event. In the stands, some people peered through binoculars, eager for the action to get started. The noise and excitement inside the dome rose as the lights dimmed. Finally, the moment they all eagerly awaited arrived. At first, the crowd roared, but soon a hush fell over the stadium. A small woman with blond hair had shyly stepped onto the stage and opened a book—her book. She started to read, bringing the familiar characters and magical world she had created to life. This was the largest crowd ever gathered for an author reading. The woman in the center of the frenzy was J. K. Rowling.

Rowling had traveled to Canada from her home in Britain, where the story of her own life began. It was a life filled with books. Stories had fed her imagination from the time she was a little girl. She read anything she could get her hands on and wrote her first story when she was six years old. Writing became her passion. During her school years, she filled notebook after notebook. Then in 1990, a few years out of college, an idea popped into her head that would change her life. She imagined a boy named Harry Potter, an orphan who learns at the age of eleven that he is a wizard.

The vision of this boy wizard inspired Rowling. During the next few years—years of marriage, divorce, teaching, single parenting, and poverty—Rowling plotted out seven novels that would tell Harry's story. In 1995 she finished the first manuscript, *Harry Potter and the Philosopher's Stone*. Twelve publishers rejected her work before one took a risk and gave her a contract to publish her book. In 1997 Rowling's dream became reality. She was a published author, one who was pleased just to visit a bookstore and see something she wrote on the shelves.

But that was only the beginning. The story of Harry Potter sparked the imaginations of people all around the planet. Children and adults alike followed Harry into a magical world, where he finds true and loyal friends, studies to be a wizard, and fights an evil villain and his followers. Rowling had produced five more novels by 2006. The success of her books is staggering. By early 2007, more than 325 million books had been sold in sixty-four languages in countries around the world. And Rowling, history's highest-paid author, had an estimated wealth of more than one billion dollars. This shy, passionate, and funny writer, who had once hoped just to see her book in print, was one of the most influential people in the world.

Rowling's influence stretches from kids who have only recently learned to read to scholars who write academic papers and hold conferences that explore her ideas. Her books have led to a greater interest in children's literature. They have also led to censorship from those who say the books promote witchcraft to children. But overwhelmingly, parents and teachers praise Rowling's messages of kindness, bravery, friendship, and the power of good over evil.

Rowling's biggest influence by far is on children, who have an intense love for her stories about Harry Potter. She remembers clearly how she felt as a child and writes from those feelings. She connects with kids and does not talk down to them. And she writes as many words as it takes to tell her story. Children are not intimidated by the thickness of her books. In fact, many kids—some of whom had never before shown an interest in reading—gladly turn off their TVs and shove aside video games to delve into Harry Potter's adventures. They wear out flashlight batteries by reading after they should be asleep. They dig into their own pockets for the money to buy a book. J. K. Rowling has created a world that invites children to explore their own imaginations. In doing so, she has accomplished what many never thought possible: she has made reading cool.

Rowling's parents lived in this home in Yate, England, when she was born.

Chapter **ONE**

A Born Storyteller

IN THE SUMMER OF **1964,** TWO DARK-HAIRED strangers boarded a train at King's Cross Station in London, England. Pete Rowling was in the Royal Navy, and Anne Volant was a member of the Women's Royal Navy Service (WRNS), called wrens. They were both eighteen years old and traveling to their new post at Arbroath, on the east coast of Scotland. Pete chose a seat next to Anne, and the two struck up a conversation. When Anne complained of being cold, Pete shared his coat. Nine hours later, Pete and Anne hopped off the train together, a couple in love.

Soon Pete and Anne decided a life in the navy was not for them. They left the service and married. Both were Londoners, used to the bustle of the city. But now the newlyweds wanted a quiet, peaceful life in the country. They found what they were looking for in Yate, a small farming and mining town near Bristol in southwestern England. The Rowlings moved into a one-story house on Sundridge Park, a gently winding street near open fields.

Although still in their teens, Pete and Anne were eager to shoulder the responsibilities of family life. Hardworking and energetic, Pete wanted a career in engineering. He found employment as an apprentice engineer on the production line at Bristol Siddeley, an aircraft engine company in Bristol. Anne settled the couple into their new home. She gardened, kept a spotless house, and prepared for the birth of their first child.

Jo and Di

On July 31, 1965, the Rowlings became a family of three when Anne gave birth to a girl at Cottage Hospital in Yate. The proud new parents called their round, light-haired daughter Joanne, and no middle name appears on her birth certificate. Soon everyone called her by her nickname—Jo.

Jo's earliest memory is of a day nearly two years later. "I distinctly remember," she said, "playing with a bit of plasticine [play dough] in the kitchen while my father rushed in and out of the room, hurrying backwards and forwards to my mother, who was giving birth in their bedroom." Jo did not recall meeting her new sister, a dark-eyed, dark-haired baby named Dianne, but she did remember eating the plasticine. Like her older sister, Dianne received only a first name, which was shortened to Di.

In the few years that the Rowlings had lived in Yate, their neighborhood had changed. Pete and Anne saw new houses and businesses filling in the open spaces that once drew them to the village. The quiet, small-town atmosphere they wanted for their new family was disappearing. When Jo was four years old, the Rowlings moved into a modern, three-bedroom house. It was on Nicholls Lane in nearby Winterbourne, a growing suburb still dotted with green fields.

LIFE IN WINTERBOURNE

The Rowlings settled into life in Winterbourne. Like many of his neighbors, Pete made the short commute to Bristol every day. He was among ten thousand workers employed at the airplane engine plant, which by this time had merged with other companies to become part of Rolls-Royce. Pete worked long days. Soon he was moving off the assembly line and into a management position.

Many children lived in the new neighborhood. Their mothers often gathered for a chat over tea while the children played in yards up and down Nicholls Lane. Among the playmates were Ian and Vikki Potter, a brother and sister whose last name Jo especially liked. She was not very fond of her own last name, which inspired all kinds of jokes from the other children about "Rowling stones" and "Rowling pins." Names fascinated Jo, and she tucked them away in her mind as she grew up.

Anne kept order in a hectic household and seemed to have endless energy. She swam, played guitar, danced to records by the Beatles, and took long walks with the family dog, Thumper. She became an expert cook who made sure her family ate meals together. "When she did stop rushing around, however," remembered Jo, "it was usually with book in hand. She would read absolutely anything: classics, airport blockbusters, biographies, historical romances, thrillers, whodunits, and so fast that my father refused to believe she hadn't skipped alternate pages." Anne's love of books rubbed off on her daughters, especially Jo.

The first book Jo remembers is *The Wind in the Willows*, by Kenneth Grahame. When she had the measles at the age of four, her father settled into a chair at her bedside and read about the animal characters Rat, Toad, Mole, and Badger and their adventures in the British countryside. Jo was captivated. "I don't remember feeling ill at all—just lying there listening to those stories," she recalled.

Jo became a storyteller, and she made Di listen. "I was much bigger than [she was] and could hold her down," Jo later joked. Most of Jo's earliest stories were about rabbits because the girls dreamed of having one for a pet. One tale involved Di falling into a hole, where the rabbit family who lived there fed her strawberries.

Jo and Di grew up fighting "like a pair of wildcats imprisoned together in a very small cage," Jo remembered. But when they were not arguing and throwing things at each other, they were best friends. Jo, who could be rather bossy, took the lead when it came to what they should do. She often directed dramatic plays based on her stories. Jo said that Di put up with this bossiness because Di always had a starring role. But in reality, Di loved Jo's imaginative tales and games.

The staircase in the sisters' Winterbourne house inspired one of their favorite games—acting out a cliff-top drama over and over again. "One of us would 'dangle' from the topmost stair, holding hands with the other and pleading with them not to let go, offering all manner of bribery and blackmail, until falling to their 'death,'" Jo remembered.

Jo started school when she was five years old. On her first day, she dressed in a red and gray uniform, and then she and her mother made the five-minute walk to Saint Michael's Church of England School. "When Mum came to pick me up for lunch," Jo remembered, "I thought that was it and that I'd 'done' school and wouldn't need to go back." But Jo grew to love her little school and so did Di when she was old enough to join her sister. Every afternoon

Anne picked up her daughters after school for the short walk home. Sometimes they took detours to the duck pond or to visit the horses and donkeys at the village stables.

During her early school years, Jo's love of stories grew even stronger. Some of her favorite books were by Richard Scarry, who wrote funny stories about the everyday antics of his animal characters. Jo called the first book she ever wrote—at the age of six—"a complete rip-off" of Richard Scarry. It was titled simply "Rabbit" and was about a character of the same name. Rabbit came down with the measles, and his friends, including a giant bumblebee named Miss Bee, stopped by to perk up his spirits. "I gave it to my mother, and she said 'That's lovely,' as a mother would, 'That's very, very good.' I stood there and thought, 'Well, get it published then.'"

A MOVE AND A LOSS

Jo turned nine years old in 1974. That same year, her parents discovered Tutshill, a small village on the border of England and Wales. Pete had always wanted to fix up an old house. So when he and Anne stumbled across Church Cottage, a stone house for sale on the edge of the village, they snatched it up and made plans to move from Winterbourne. Just a half-hour drive from Bristol, Tutshill is located between the River Wye and River Severn and near the oaks, beeches, and pines of an ancient forest called the Forest of Dean. The Rowlings had a breathtaking view from their new home.

Built in 1848, Church Cottage had been the village school until a larger school was needed. It stood next to Saint Luke's Church and its cemetery. "All our friends thought it was spooky living next to a grave-yard," remembered Jo, "but we liked it. I still love graveyards—they are a great source of names." Only

The Rowlings lived next to Saint Luke's Church in Tutshill, England.

yards away, on the other side of Church Cottage, stood Jo and Di's new school, Tutshill Church of England Primary School.

When the fall term started, Jo found herself seated in a small, old-fashioned classroom dressed in a crisp blue uniform. Jo's new teacher, Sylvia Morgan, was very stern. She terrified Jo. Mrs. Morgan's first task for the class was a math test. Jo, who had not yet learned fractions, did not get a single answer right. Mrs. Morgan sorted her students by how smart she thought they were. Those she believed to be bright sat on her left and those she thought less smart on her right. "It took me a few days to realize I was in the 'stupid' row," Jo recalled. "I was as far right as you could get without sitting in the playground."

Jo's early days in Tutshill became more difficult when Kathleen Rowling died suddenly of a heart attack. Jo adored her grandmother, Kathleen Rowling. It had always been a treat for Jo and Di to stay with her and their grandfather, Ernie. The couple ran a grocery store and lived above it. During visits, the girls spent hours playing shop with real cans of food and real money. Jo would be the shopkeeper, and Di would be the customer.

The girls' other grandparents were Stanley and Frieda Volant. Jo recalled that Stanley was "a great dreamer, and spent a lot of time in his garden shed, making things." Frieda was a dog lover who seemed to prefer her four-legged friends to people.

Jo soon settled into her new life and her new school in Tutshill. She and Di often went exploring in the fields and along the River Wye. They also joined a club called the Brownies that taught girls about safety, first aid, and community service. The Brownies often planned special events such as Christmas and Halloween parties for the elderly in the village. At school Jo had proved to her teacher that she was a good student. By the end of the school year, Mrs. Morgan had moved Jo from her seat on the right to one on the left. But this shift had one big downside. "Mrs. Morgan made me swap seats with my best friend, so that in one short walk across the room I became clever but unpopular," Jo later recalled.

The Rowlings' home was called Church Cottage.

Chapter **TWO**

A BURNING
AMBITION

BECAUSE JO AND DI WERE SO CLOSE IN AGE, PEOPLE
often compared them to one another. With her dark-
haired good looks, Di was known as the pretty and
lively sister. Jo, who had reddish hair and thick
glasses that perched on her freckly face, was the
quiet, serious, and studious one. She was insecure
and worried a lot, but she acted confident to cover it
up. "I always felt I had to achieve, my hand always
had to be the first to go up, I always had to be
right," Jo said. "Maybe it was because I felt quite
plain in comparison to my sister. I probably felt I
had to compensate."

Books filled the nooks and crannies of Church Cottage, and they continued to play a central role in Jo's

life. She would read anything she could get her hands on, and her parents were happy to provide a steady supply. Her favorite book, *The Little White Horse* by Elizabeth Goudge, was about a plain-looking orphan girl who goes to live with her uncle in his English manor. Jo also loved *Black Beauty, Little Women, I Capture the Castle,* and books in the *Chronicles of Narnia* series by C. S. Lewis. By the age of nine, she was delving into adult fare, including Ian Fleming's novels about the British spy James Bond.

These books and others inspired Jo to work on her own writing. She spent more time developing characters and creating detailed plots. One of her early efforts was an adventure story titled "The Seven Cursed Diamonds." "I always, always wanted to be a writer but I *never* shared my burning ambition with anyone," remembered Jo. Although she did not share her dream, Jo did show her stories to Di, who always encouraged her to keep writing.

WYEDEAN COMPREHENSIVE SCHOOL

Jo started to lose some of her seriousness in her early teenage years. By this time, she and her sister had both donned the yellow and brown uniform of Wyedean Comprehensive, a public high school in the nearby village of Sedbury. Jo quickly fell into a group of smart and studious friends who spent their lunch periods listening to her tell soap opera-type stories. "They usually involved us all doing heroic and daring deeds we certainly wouldn't have done in real life; we were all too swotty [nerdy]," Jo recalled.

Although she lacked talent in what she considered "practical" subjects such as metalworking, woodworking, and gym, Jo received high marks from her English teachers for her imaginative writing. Her favorite English teacher, Lucy Shepherd, was an inspiration. Miss Shepherd cared about her students' progress and had high expectations. "I really respected her because she was a teacher who was passionate about teaching us. She was an introduction to a different kind of woman, I suppose. She was a feminist, and clever," Jo recalled. From Miss Shepherd, Jo learned the importance of structure and pacing in her writing. She began to make her writing more precise. "I learned a lot from her," Jo said. "She was the only teacher I ever confided in. She inspired trust."

Books continued to influence Jo. She loved the novels of nineteenth-century author Jane Austen, whose main characters were often sisters dealing with the expectations and constraints of England's upper-class society. She read Austen's *Emma* again and again. She also read William Makepeace Thackeray's *Vanity Fair.* But it was Jessica Mitford's autobiographical work, *Hons and Rebels,* that inspired Jo most. Her great-aunt Ivy told her about Mitford, who had run away from her wealthy family, bought a camera, and gone traveling. Jo was fascinated by this rebel and admired her adventurous spirit. "She had tremendous moral courage and did some physically brave things as a human rights activist. I love her sense of humor, her great independence," Jo later said.

DIFFICULT NEWS

After both of her daughters had started at Wyedean, Anne Rowling took a job as a laboratory assistant in the school's chemistry department. She enjoyed working with the beakers and chemicals and found particular delight in being around the students. The job also gave her time with her daughters as the threesome made the trip to and from school each day.

Around this time, Anne started having trouble lifting the teapot. She sometimes felt the pricks of "pins and needles" in her right arm. Other times it felt numb and weak. At first, Anne dismissed the feeling as minor aches and pains, but within a few years, the pain had spread. She was thirty-five years old when her doctor told her she had multiple sclerosis (MS), an incurable disease that attacks the nervous system. The severity and timing of the attacks are unpredictable. People who have MS can experience loss of balance, numbness, weakness, fatigue, and loss of vision. Most people with MS go through long periods of recovery, but some can become seriously disabled in a short amount of time.

Anne did not have those long periods of recovery. Her condition grew slowly but steadily worse. At the age of fifteen, Jo found the news of her mother's health hard to grasp. "I think most people believe, deep down, that their mothers are indestructible; it was a terrible shock to hear that she had an incurable illness, but even then, I did not fully realize what the diagnosis might mean," Jo recalled. In fact, Anne cheerfully carried on, working hard to keep life at Church Cottage unchanged. The house was as clean as ever, and she kept up her job at Wyedean Comprehensive for as long as she could.

Despite Anne's efforts, there was a general feeling of sadness at Church Cottage. It was hard for Jo to be at home, so she turned to her friends for comfort and escape. She also delved deeper into her studies. During her last years at Wyedean, she was focusing on her English classes and her studies in French and German. She saw her first live performance of a play, *King Lear* by William Shakespeare, during a class trip to Stratford-upon-Avon.

Jo became more interested in music too. "I played the acoustic guitar and would fantasize about playing an electric guitar solo," she remembered. Jo had always liked the Beatles and became a big fan of the punk band the Clash. She adopted a punk style, which included wearing heavy, black eye-makeup—a look she would keep for a decade. She and her friends went to the occasional dances offered to area teens. But the general lack of excitement in a rural village like Tutshill often made Jo bored and restless.

FINDING FREEDOM

Jo found a cure for her boredom in Sean Harris, a boy who started at Wyedean during her last year. Sean had been living in Cyprus, an island in the Mediterranean Sea, where his father was stationed in the army. He and Jo became instant and loyal friends. Unlike Jo, Sean knew how to drive, and he had a turquoise and white Ford Anglia that gave the two friends freedom from parents and the dullness of rural life. They hit the highways to find fun in the clubs and discos of Bristol, Newport, and other bigger towns. "Some of the happiest memories of my teenage years involve zooming off into the darkness in Sean's car," Jo remembered.

She felt she could share her hopes and dreams with Sean. "He was the first person with whom I really discussed my serious ambition to be a writer and he was also the only person who thought I was bound to be a success at it, which meant much more to me than I ever told him at the time," Jo recalled.

During her last year at Wyedean, Jo continued to earn outstanding grades and was popular with her classmates. They even voted her head girl. The head girl is a representative for her school and helps monitor younger students. By this time, Jo was making decisions about her future. Though her greatest ambition was to be a writer, she also had a strong desire to fight for social change like her idol,

Rowling looked up to Jessica Mitford, left, a writer and activist.

Jessica Mitford. Most of all, Jo wanted to get out into the world and away from tiny Tutshill. Her parents convinced her to major in a foreign language in college, a practical pursuit that could lead to a steady job as a bilingual secretary. So after graduating with honors from Wyedean in 1983, Jo left behind her quiet life at Church Cottage and set out for the University of Exeter.

JESSICA MITFORD

You may not be able to change the world, but at least you can embarrass the guilty.

—Jessica Mitford

Jessica Mitford was born in 1917 and raised as a member of the nobility in Great Britain. While her brother attended top schools, she and her five sisters received their education from their mother. At the age of nineteen, Mitford ran away to marry Esmond Romilly, a man she admired for fighting the Fascists in Spain during the Spanish Civil War (1936–1939).

Mitford was fiercely opposed to Fascism, a political movement that favored a government led by a dictator who has unlimited power. She was appalled when her sister Diana married the head of the British Fascist movement and her sister Unity became an aquaintance of Adolf Hitler, the German dictator. By this time, Mitford and her husband had emigrated from Great Britain to the United States. Romilly became a soldier in World War II (1939–1945) and was killed in combat in 1941.

Mitford went to work in a government office, became active in the United Federal Workers Union, and joined the Communist Party. Communists support a type of government that controls the economy and works to share all goods equally among the people. In 1943 Mitford married lawyer Robert Treuhaft—also a member of the Communist Party—and settled in Oakland, California. Together, Mitford and her husband worked in support of civil rights through the party's Civil Rights Congress.

Mitford then turned to writing, publishing her autobiography, *Hons* [honorables or nobility] *and Rebels* in 1960. *The American Way of Death*, a book exposing fraud in the funeral industry, came next. Known for her charm and wit, she soon gained fame as a journalist who would dig up the truth and root out injustices. In other books, she took on the U.S. prison system and medical regulators. She continued to write until her death in 1996. Mitford is remembered for inspiring political activists around the world.

Jo attended Exeter University. The campus features historical buildings set among gardens and forested hills.

A NEW WORLD

Although the University of Exeter on the southern coast of England was only a two-hour drive from her home in Tutshill, the campus was a whole new world to Jo. The dorm where she took up residence was small and cramped. And she found herself just one of many students who had been smart and popular in their hometown schools. Suddenly, she was nervous and unsure of herself. "At first Exeter was a bit of a shock," Jo said. "I was expecting to be amongst lots of similar people. . . . But it wasn't like that. However, once I'd made friends with some like-minded people I began to enjoy myself."

Jo met many of her friends at Devonshire House, Exeter's student union. She became a regular at the coffee bar there, which was a good place for conversation. And she and her friends sometimes ventured out to the pubs in the evenings. Relishing the freedom of college life, shy Jo became more outgoing among her friends. She dated and soon had a serious boyfriend, but she also enjoyed the camaraderie of her female friends. As she had at Wyedean, Jo told stories that featured her new friends as the main characters. And music was as important as ever. About this time, Jo discovered the Smiths, a band that quickly became her all-time favorite group. She would try to pick out the band's rather sad melodies on her guitar.

Jo studied French at Exeter, which she later decided was a big mistake. "I wanted to do English but felt everyone would say: 'What use is that?' Although I longed to be a writer, I never thought it would be possible, so told only my close friends," Jo said. She continued to write stories and even dabbled in poetry, but she has admitted that she could have worked harder at her studies. Jo was no longer the academic standout that she had been at Wyedean. Instead, she had become an average student who was known to be something of a disorganized daydreamer.

There were many bright spots in Jo's studies at Exeter. One was learning about the classical literature of ancient Greece and Rome. The mythology and history of this period sparked her imagination. And studying French meant that she was required to spend a year in France to learn about the culture and immerse herself in the language. She flung herself into work on the dissertation she had to write to earn her degree. It was a three-thousand-word paper in French. Throughout her college years, Jo fed her mind with more books, among them *A Tale of Two Cities* by Charles Dickens and J. R. R. Tolkien's *Lord of the Rings* trilogy. By the time she graduated in 1987, Jo had racked up some hefty fines for overdue books at the university library.

Rowling moved to London in 1987.

Chapter **THREE**

THE BOY WIZARD

AFTER LEAVING EXETER, ROWLING MOVED TO LONDON to find a career. She took a secretarial course for people skilled in languages. Then, inspired by Jessica Mitford's activism, Rowling accepted a job as a research assistant for Amnesty International. This organization works to protect human rights around the world. Rowling helped research cases of human rights abuse in French-speaking African countries. Although she found her work interesting, she did not think she was very good at it. She was too disorganized. Also, writing drew her attention away from her work. She had started a novel for adults and stole every spare minute she could to work on it. Whenever her coworkers asked her to lunch, she made excuses and raced off to a café, where she would scrawl some notes or plot out a chapter. Cafés became her favorite places to write.

After two years at Amnesty International, Rowling was feeling frustrated. She was tired of working behind the scenes. She wanted to be where the action was, on the front lines in the fight for social justice. But there were no opportunities for her then. She resigned and drifted from one secretarial job to another. For a brief time, she worked for a publisher typing letters to authors whose manuscripts were rejected. She also abandoned one novel she was writing and went on to another, neither of which she thought good enough to publish.

Rowling became a fast typist. But in all other areas, she proved to be "the worst secretary ever." To her, being a secretary was just a way to support herself while she worked on her writing. "All I ever liked about working in offices was being able to type up stories on the computer when no one was looking," Rowling said. "I was never paying much attention in meetings because I was usually scribbling bits of my latest stories in the margins of the pad, or choosing excellent names for the characters. This is a problem when you are supposed to be taking the minutes of the meeting."

AN IDEA

In 1990 Rowling decided to follow a boyfriend to Manchester, a large industrial city in northern England.

She began spending weekends there, searching for an apartment. At the end of one weekend in June, she was returning home to London by train. As she watched the countryside go by, the image of a dark-haired boy suddenly popped into her mind. He was scrawny, with green eyes, round glasses, and a lightning-bolt-shaped mark that streaked across his forehead. The boy was a wizard, but he didn't know it yet. He would learn to be a wizard at a wizarding school. "It was the purest stroke of inspiration I've ever had in my life," Rowling later said.

She immediately reached for a pen and paper, but she found she did not have either with her. Her shyness kept her from borrowing the materials from fellow passengers. Although Rowling was frustrated at the time, she later decided this was a stroke of good luck. Instead of jotting down her immediate thoughts, she closed her eyes and followed her racing imagination. "I think that perhaps if I had had to slow down the ideas so that I could capture them on paper I might have stifled some of them," Rowling later noted. The train broke down midway to London, which gave her four straight hours to get acquainted with the boy she would later name Harry Potter.

First, Rowling thought about where he would go to school. It would be an imposing and mysterious castle—the perfect place to train young witches and wizards. In her mind, this school, which she later named Hogwarts School of Witchcraft and Wizardry,

By the time Rowling's train arrived into King's Cross railway station, she had started planning her story about a boy wizard.

needed to be located in a secluded place. She set it in the rugged landscape of northern Scotland. Rowling was familiar with many ancient castles, including one near Church Cottage in Tutshill. But, she said, "I have never seen a castle anywhere that looks the way I imagine Hogwarts." By the time she stepped off the train at King's Cross station in London, she knew she would write seven books—one for each year the boy wizard went to school at Hogwarts. In addition to Harry Potter, Rowling had dreamed up his friend Ron Weasley, the school

gamekeeper Hagrid, and two of the school's ghosts—
Peeves and Nearly Headless Nick.

Rowling set to work on her new idea that very
night. "I spent a lot of time inventing the rules for
the magical world so that I knew the limits of
magic," Rowling later noted. "Then I had to invent
the different ways wizards could accomplish certain
things. Some of the magic in the books is based on
what people used to believe really worked, but most
of it is my invention." Rowling saw all this planning
as research. She had to find out who Harry Potter
was. His parents, who had lived in the wizarding
world, had died, but how? And why didn't Harry
know he was a wizard? How had he come to live
with his nonmagical aunt and uncle? And what would
happen to him during his years at Hogwarts? Rowling
would spend five years figuring out the answers to
these questions and many more.

CHARACTERS FIRST

The characters came first. Rowling wrote a life history
for nearly all of them. She knew she could not put
this vast amount of information in her books, but she
felt she needed to know her characters inside out
before writing about them. Next came the names.
After years of collecting unusual names, Rowling had
plenty to pluck out of her mind for her characters—
and she kept hunting for more. Nothing pleased her
as much as looking over a long list of names. "For me

it's like casting an eye over a pile of unwrapped presents, each of the names representing a whole person. War memorials, telephone directories, shop fronts, saints, villains, baby-naming books—you name it, I've got names from it!" Rowling later said.

Rowling developed the characters and setting for Harry Potter's adventures before starting to write the story. Pictured here is the Hogwarts Express from the set of one of the Harry Potter movies.

It did not take long to find a name for her main character. "Harry" had always been one of Rowling's favorite boy's names. His last name, however, took a little longer. She tried out several surnames before choosing "Potter," the last name of her childhood friends in Winterbourne. Harry Potter is famous in the magical world as "the boy who lived." When he was just a baby, the dark wizard Voldemort destroyed his house and killed his parents, James and Lily Potter. Harry survived the attack. Voldemort was so weakened after trying to kill Harry that he retreated. The only remaining evidence of the event is the lightning-bolt-shaped scar that Voldemort's wand left on Harry's forehead. As Harry learns about his past and the magical world, he must also deal with the added pressure of fame.

Rowling put some of herself into Harry. They share the same birthday—July 31. Harry tends to be quiet and serious, just as Rowling was as a child. She imagined Harry as a bit of an old soul, someone who has a depth of wisdom and understanding beyond his years. He is also sensible, a loyal friend, and very brave, a trait Rowling admires more than any other. Unlike Rowling, Harry is good at sports, especially the popular wizarding game Quidditch. At Hogwarts he is just an average student who does not work as hard as he could. He is naturally good at some subjects (Defense Against the Dark Arts) and completely awful at others (Potions). And like everyone, Harry has faults. He can be proud, stubborn, self-involved, and impulsive.

Harry's best friend, Ron Weasley, keeps him grounded. As Rowling wrote about Ron, she realized that he was much like her friend Sean Harris. "Although I never meant him to be like Sean, once I got Ron onto the page he often behaved like my oldest friend, who is both very funny and deeply loyal," she said. In many ways, Ron has a life Harry has always wanted. He is a typical boy who grew up with two doting parents, Arthur and Molly Weasley. Ron has a younger sister, Ginny, and five older brothers—Bill, Charlie, Percy, and the prankster twins, Fred and George. The Weasley children all have one thing in common—red hair. Being the youngest of six brothers, Ron often feels overshadowed by their accomplishments. He seems to be mediocre at everything and struggles to find the one thing that he is good at, the talent that will set him apart from his siblings. The Weasleys' lack of money often embarrasses Ron, whose clothes and belongings are usually worn hand-me-downs. But he has a home full of love, laughter, and happy chaos, something Harry longs for.

The character of Hermione Granger rounds out the trio of friends who are at the center of Rowling's story. Rowling had carried around the name Hermione since she first saw a character of that name in Shakespeare's play *The Winter's Tale*. At first, Hermione Granger had the last name Puckle, but Rowling decided such an intelligent and ambitious girl needed a surname that better reflected her serious

Rowling poses with the actors who play Ron, left, *Harry,* center right, *and Hermione,* right, *in movies based on the* Harry Potter *books.*

nature. Hermione is plain looking and has brown hair and brown eyes. An only child, she comes from a supportive, nonmagical family. Hermione has a great fear of failure. So she studies hard, determined to be the best and brightest student at Hogwarts. Hermione is often an annoying know-it-all, who lectures her friends and openly expresses her disapproval when they do something wrong. But she is also kind-hearted, clever, and loyal. Of all the characters, Hermione is the most like Rowling herself. "Hermione is me, near enough. A caricature of me when I was younger," Rowling later said. "I wasn't that clever. But I was that annoying on occasion."

Harry would be the hero of Rowling's story, but he would need Ron and Hermione's support to get through his years at Hogwarts. The bonds of friendship among these three characters would be vital to the story. And their courage, their faith in one another, and their belief in the power of good over evil would be important themes.

HARRY'S TWO WORLDS

Soon Rowling had boxes crammed with notes on her new project, and they bulged more each day. Rowling's notes traveled with her as she made the move to Manchester and settled into a new job. She took a secretarial position with the Manchester Chamber of Commerce.

With work, spending time with her boyfriend, and learning her way around a new city, Rowling could not give her full attention to her writing. But she spent every spare moment creating Harry Potter's world. Her hero would actually straddle two worlds—the magical world and the parallel world of the Muggles, the name she gave to regular, nonmagical people. The orphaned Harry would be raised until the age of eleven by his Muggle aunt and uncle, Vernon and Petunia Dursley. In the Muggle world, everything is clean and orderly. The well-kept houses with their well-groomed lawns line up side by side along quiet streets. Muggles rarely vary their daily routines. Any-one who looks or behaves out of the ordinary raises eyebrows. And there is hardly ever any excitement.

In contrast, there is a surprise around every corner in the wizarding world. Nothing seems orderly. Houses, buildings, and roads go every which way. People and objects appear and disappear. The people in paintings and photographs wander in and out of view, and mirrors sometimes talk. Ghosts, giants, and elves live among the witches and wizards, who cast spells, create magic potions, and fly broom-sticks. Goblins run banks. Owls deliver the daily mail. Unicorns, dragons, and centaurs live in the wild. Beneath all of these wonders, there is a con-stant sense of danger and excitement.

Even wizarding sports have an element of danger. Huge crowds gather to watch matches of Quidditch, a fast-paced, airborne game played on brooms. Rowling invented the game after having a spat with her boyfriend. "I stormed out of the house, went to the pub—and invented Quidditch," she later recalled.

Rowling also imagined the food in the magical world. There are chocolate frogs that come with col-lectible cards of famous wizards. There are jelly beans in every flavor, including liver, grass, vomit, and ear-wax. There is butterbeer, a flavorful drink that warms you from the inside out. At Hogwarts every meal is like a feast. Course after course of delicious dishes—roasts, sausages, potatoes, vegetables, puddings, and desserts—magically appear on plates, which are refilled until students have had enough to eat.

Witches and wizards move back and forth between their world and the parallel Muggle world. Often dressed in capes and other somewhat odd clothing, they attract stares and looks of disapproval from Muggles. "The wizards represent all that the true 'Muggle' most fears: They are plainly outcasts and comfortable with being so. Nothing is more unnerving to the truly conventional than the unashamed misfit!" Rowling later said. In the magical world, there are strict rules about the use of magic around Muggles. Rowling envisioned a governing body called the Ministry of Magic that enforces these rules. But keeping the magical world hidden from the Muggles is difficult. Witches and wizards need to be on guard.

CREATING HOGWARTS

Rowling's vision of Hogwarts—the main setting of each book—started taking shape. Students travel to the school on a train called the Hogwarts Express. When they arrive, they find an enormous stone castle. Perched on a high cliff, the school overlooks a large lake and an enchanted forest. Mountains surround the castle, which is often shrouded in fog.

Hogwarts looks as mysterious on the inside as it does on the outside. Torches cast light and shadow on the mazelike interior. Ghosts such as Peeves, Nearly Headless Nick, the Bloody Baron, and Moaning Myrtle haunt all corners of the school. Rooms appear and disappear. Staircases change direction without warning. Doors sometimes will not open without a polite request. The Great Hall, where the students gather for meals and celebrations, has a ceiling that is bewitched to look like the sky. Dark dungeons and chambers make up the lower levels of the school, while towers with amazing views rise into the air.

Four famous wizards established Hogwarts long ago, and students belong to one of four houses named for these founders. Harry, Ron, and Hermione are in Gryffindor, the house known for its daring and brave wizards. Hufflepuffs are said to be hardworking and loyal, while Ravenclaws are wise and witty. Cunning and sly students belong to Slytherin House, which has produced many dark wizards, including Voldemort. Harry's biggest rival, the sinister bully Draco Malfoy, is a Slytherin. Each house has its own common room and dormitories guarded by a painting whose subject keeps the password needed to enter.

Despite its chaotic appearance, Hogwarts is a place of order and rules. Its motto, "Never Tickle a Sleeping Dragon," cautions students that breaking the rules could lead to unexpected trouble or danger. Students must answer for their actions to the headmaster, professors, and staff. The headmaster of Hogwarts is Albus Dumbledore, a kind, wise, and extremely powerful wizard who is feared by Voldemort. "Dumbledore, which means 'bumblebee' in Old English,

ADVICE TO ASPIRING WRITERS

J.K. Rowling always knew she wanted to be a writer, and she feels fortunate that she can make a living doing what she does best. But her success took planning, hard work, dedication—and luck. When aspiring young writers ask her for advice, here is what she tells them: "Read as much as you can. Keep writing and throwing it away until one day you do something that you don't think belongs in the [trash] bin. Stick to writing what you know about. Don't give up."

seemed to suit the headmaster because one of his passions is music, and I imagined him walking around humming to himself," Rowling later said. Professor Dumbledore is Harry's main protector. The head of Gryffindor House, Professor Minerva McGonagall, teaches transfiguration—the art of changing an object from one form to another. Strict, clever, and fair, she is someone Harry, Ron, and Hermione trust and respect.

The one professor they have no trust in is Severus Snape, their Potions teacher and the head of Slytherin House. Rowling took his last name from a village called Snape that she found on a map of Britain. Once a Death Eater, as supporters of Voldemort are called, Professor Snape has a strong dislike for Harry. Although Dumbledore trusts Snape, Harry and his friends have their suspicions about him. Another teacher is Professor Binns, a ghost who teaches History of Magic. Professor Sprout gives instruction in Herbology, where students learn about the powers of magical plants. And a tiny wizard named Professor Flitwick teaches Charms.

Rubeus Hagrid is the adult that Harry, Ron, and Hermione go to for comfort, information, and advice. Hagrid is part giant and speaks in the West Country accent heard in the region where Rowling grew up. He lives in a cabin on the school grounds and watches over the magical creatures in Hogwarts' Forbidden Forest. Hagrid has a way with these creatures, but he sometimes overlooks their danger to others. Hagrid becomes a treasured friend to Harry, Ron, and Hermione. Rowling has admitted that Hagrid was one of her favorite characters and that she had a great affection for him.

As 1990 progressed, Rowling's mind continued to overflow with ideas for her characters and the magical world she had created for them. But she kept her new project and her excitement about it to herself, as usual.

Rowling moved to Porto, Portugal, in 1991, to teach English.

Chapter **FOUR**

A Change of Scenery

SHORTLY BEFORE CHRISTMAS **1990,** ROWLING traveled home for a visit with her parents in Tutshill. She noticed that her mother was extremely tired and very thin. By this time, the MS had advanced so far that Anne needed a wheelchair to get around outside the house. Indoors, she was unable to go upstairs and used a walker to get around the ground floor of Church Cottage.

On Christmas Eve, Rowling said good-bye to her parents and returned to Manchester. She planned to spend the rest of the holidays with her boyfriend and his family. Then on December 30, the phone rang early in the morning. When she heard her father's voice, Rowling knew he had bad news. Her mother had died. Although Rowling had seen how weak her mother was, her death was unexpected. "I don't know how I didn't realize how ill she was, except that I had watched her deteriorate for so long that the change, at the time, didn't seem so dramatic," Rowling remembered. Anne was only forty-five years old when she died.

Rowling's world had suddenly changed, and the months to follow were a terrible time in her life. "I remember feeling as though there was a [chunk of pavement] pressing down upon my chest, a literal pain in my heart," said Rowling. Twenty-five years old and crushed with grief, Rowling felt overwhelmed by everyday life. Her job at the Chamber of Commerce suddenly ended. She did not like the new position she found at the University of Manchester. Her relationship with her boyfriend was falling apart. And then came the last straw. Rowling's home was robbed, and the thieves stole everything her mother had left her. She decided it was time to get away.

PORTO

In the newspaper, Rowling found a small advertisement placed by a school in Porto, Portugal, that was looking for English teachers. She applied for a job, got it, and was off to a warmer climate, eager for a new challenge and a change of scenery. Located in northern Portugal on the mouth of the Douro River, Porto is the country's second largest city and a center of industry. The variety of architecture in its churches, palaces, and bridges makes Porto one of Portugal's most beautiful cities.

Rowling moved into a large, four-bedroom apartment that the school's principal reserved for teachers. She became instant friends with her new roommates, Aine Kiely from Ireland and another teacher from England, Jill Prewett. The three taught in the evenings and afterward found fun at the local bars or discos or met for conversation over dinners of pizza and wine.

Rowling enjoyed teaching English. Her students ranged in age from eight to sixty-two. Some were businesspeople who wanted to further their careers, while others took lessons for fun. There were also students who needed help passing exams. These teenagers, who were bubbling with ideas and opinions, were Rowling's favorites.

Working evenings meant that Rowling had her days free to write. She sat in the cafés of Porto, sipping strong coffee and working on her novel in longhand. By this time, she had started drafting her story about Harry Potter. Since her mother's death, however, there had been some changes in her young hero. "Harry's feelings about his dead parents had become much deeper, much more real," Rowling said.

During her first weeks in Porto, she wrote what would become her favorite chapter of the book—"The Mirror of Erised." When Harry looks into this enchanted mirror, he sees not only himself but also

Rowling loved to write in cafés.

his parents and other relatives standing behind him, smiling, waving, and looking proud. The word *erised* spelled backwards is *desire*, and in that mirror, Harry saw that which his heart most longed for—his family. "I only fully realized upon re-reading the book how many of my own feelings about losing my mother I had given Harry," Rowling later said.

FINDING LOVE

One Saturday night, Rowling and her roommates went to a bar called the Meia Cava, where they could listen to jazz music. A Portuguese journalism student named Jorge Arantes was also there with his friends. When Rowling walked into the bar, her blue eyes immediately drew his attention. He spoke English well and struck up a conversation. They found that they both had a love of books. When Rowling learned that Arantes had read *Sense and Sensibility* by Jane Austen, one of her favorite writers, she was impressed.

Arantes called her a few days later, and they began dating. Soon they were inseparable. Within a few weeks, Rowling moved in with Arantes and his mother, Marília Rodrigues, who came to think of her son's new girlfriend as part of the family. Rowling seemed happy in her new relationship, happier than she had been since her mother's death. She told Arantes about her novel and shared the beginnings of the book with him. He recognized her talent and remembers telling her that he was in love with a great writer.

In August 1992, Arantes proposed to Rowling, and she accepted. But the couple's romance was showing signs of trouble. They often bickered, and small spats grew into big fights. Still, their plans to marry did not change. Rowling's sister Di flew in from Edinburgh, Scotland, for the wedding. And on the morning of October 16, Rowling and Arantes married in a small civil ceremony in Porto. There was no honeymoon. In fact, Rowling went to work as usual that evening. Within a few weeks, Rowling became pregnant. She taught throughout her pregnancy and continued to work on Harry Potter at local cafés. On July 27, 1993, Rowling gave birth to a healthy baby girl. She was named Jessica, after Jessica Mitford, and she became the best thing in Rowling's life. "I was over the moon to be a mother," she remembered.

BREAKING UP

Marriage and the birth of their daughter did not improve Rowling and Arantes's relationship. In fact, there was more stress than ever in their lives. Arantes had recently finished eight months of required service in the Portuguese army and had not found a job. Rowling was the sole supporter of the family. The demands of caring for a newborn baby were immense. Rowling and Arantes were both frustrated with their lives. The couple often had big arguments. Sometimes the fighting became physical.

In November 1993, their relationship reached a breaking point. Rowling told Arantes that she did not love him anymore. He exploded with anger and forced Rowling out of the house. She was left standing alone in the street with nothing. She knew that she had to get her four-month-old daughter and leave, but she feared that Arantes would keep Jessica from her. Rowling went to her old roommates for help. They called another friend, a Portuguese woman named Maria Inês Aguiar. Aguiar persuaded the police to accompany her to Arantes's house. The officers could not force Arantes to hand over Jessica, but their presence convinced him to give up the baby.

Two weeks later, Rowling and her daughter were on a flight bound for London. Her immediate thought had been to get away from Portugal and put distance between herself and her husband. But she did not have a home or a job, and she had very little money. All her possessions fit in two suitcases. She thought about going back to London, where many of her friends lived. But they were all enjoying single, carefree lives, so London did not feel like the right place for her. Her father had moved away from her childhood home in Tutshill to settle with his new wife, Janet Gallivan, in nearby Chepstow. So Rowling decided to board a train heading north to Edinburgh, where her sister Di lived with her husband, Roger Moore, a restaurant owner.

Many feelings were brewing inside Rowling, but most of all, she felt angry with herself. She had left Britain in search of a better and happier life. She was returning with her life in even more turmoil. "I never expected to find myself in that situation, and I was furious with myself," she later recalled. "But I certainly never regretted leaving, and I never ever for a second regretted Jessica. She kept me going."

After she left Portugal, Rowling made her home in Edinburgh, Scotland.

Chapter **FIVE**

THE POVERTY
TRAP

WHEN ROWLING ARRIVED IN EDINBURGH, SHE HAD a good feeling about the city. Edinburgh is Scotland's cultural center and the country's second largest city. It seemed like a place where she could be happy, a good place to bring up a child. Rowling knew it would be hard to build a new life and raise Jessica on her own. It might take a few months, but she was certain that she would soon be on firmer footing. After all, she was well educated and willing to work hard.

ENDLESS HUMILIATIONS

Unwilling to be a burden to her sister, Rowling decided to go on public assistance, government help with money for food and housing, while she looked for a job. On December 21, 1994, she made her way to the Department of Social Security, where she filled out endless paperwork. The experience was disheartening. "You have to be interviewed and explain to a lot of strangers how you came to be penniless and the sole carer of your child," Rowling later described. "I know that nobody was setting out to make me feel humiliated and worthless, though that is exactly how I felt." Her application was accepted, which meant that she would receive housing benefits and £69 ($103.50) per week to pay for food, clothing, and other needs.

Rowling put down a deposit on an apartment and bought some essentials with her remaining savings. She soon discovered that there were mice living in her walls. It was a miserable place, but she was determined to make the best of it. She endured the humiliation of signing for her public assistance check at the post office each week. She browsed in children's clothing stores in order to pick up some of the diapers offered for free in the changing room. And there were days when Jessica ate, but Rowling did not.

The day came when Rowling realized she had hit rock bottom. She was visiting a friend of her sister who had a son just a few months older than Jessica. Unlike her baby, this boy had a beautiful bedroom full of toys. "At that point, when I packed Jessica's toys away, they fitted into a shoebox, literally. I came home and cried my eyes out," Rowling remembered. She could no longer bear the noisy scratching of the mice in the walls. "I just never expected to mess up so badly that I would find myself in an unheated, mouse-infested flat [apartment], looking after my daughter. And I was angry because I felt I was letting her down," Rowling later said. So she turned to Sean Harris, who had remained a loyal friend through the years. He lent her the money she needed to move into a one-bedroom apartment in a better neighborhood.

Rowling wanted to work part-time. She soon realized, however, that she was stuck in a poverty trap. She could not work unless she found child care for Jessica, but she could not afford child care unless she had a well-paying job. Government programs were available to assist those who needed help with child care, but Rowling did not qualify. Those programs were for children "at risk," something Jessica was not because Rowling was taking good care of her. "I had naively supposed the system would be geared to helping those determined to support themselves and their children. How much I had to learn," Rowling recalled.

WRITING AGAIN

The daily struggles she faced sent Rowling into a depression. Her situation was a huge blow to her self-confidence. Rowling turned to Di when she needed comfort and a distraction from her troubles. Di's upbeat personality lifted her older sister's spirits. During one visit, Rowling mentioned her latest writing project to her sister. As usual, Di wanted to hear all about it. Rowling handed her the three chapters of the book that she had completed, and Di eagerly absorbed her sister's words. When Di smiled and then laughed out loud, Rowling was relieved. It was exactly the reaction she had been hoping for.

With words of encouragement from Di ringing in her ears, Rowling made two decisions. First, she would write the novel about Harry Potter, and then she would go to work full-time. Rowling had set her mind on teaching again, but she found that her experience did not qualify her to teach in Scotland's schools. First, she would need to earn a postgraduate certificate of education. The yearlong program would keep her busy, so she knew that if she did not write the book before she started school, she might never complete it. "And so I set to work in a kind of frenzy, determined to finish the book and at least try to get it published," Rowling said.

Every day, she and Jessica set out for a nearby park, where the fresh air and activity lulled her daughter to sleep. Then Rowling pushed the baby carriage to a café and went to work, scribbling the book out in longhand. Her favorite place to write was Nicolson's, a café co-owned by her brother-in-law. Rowling felt comfortable at Nicolson's. She could sit there undisturbed for hours, with an espresso, while Jessica napped. In the evenings, when the baby had settled down to sleep for the night, Rowling returned to the novel again. At times, she became frustrated. "Sometimes I hated the book, even while I loved it," she recalled.

The only major interruption to her writing arrived in the form of her husband. Jorge Arantes had traveled to Edinburgh from Porto in search of his wife and daughter. After Rowling left him, Arantes had turned to drugs. Rowling worried that he would become verbally and physically abusive. She was concerned about her own well-being as well as Jessica's. In March 1994, she filed papers in court asking for an action of interdict, a type of restraining order that would prevent Arantes from seeing his wife and daughter in Edinburgh. The court granted a temporary interdict, and Arantes returned to Portugal. Five months later, Rowling filed for a divorce, which would become final in June 1995. At that time, the interdict would also become permanent. "Although things were hard," she later said, "I don't regret the marriage because it gave me my daughter and I would not want to change anything about her."

Making Plans

By the end of 1994, things were starting to look up for Rowling. She was making great progress on Harry Potter. She also found a little typing work, which brought in £15 ($22.50) per week. This was the maximum salary she was allowed to earn without reducing the amount of her public assistance check.

With the end of her novel in sight, Rowling started making plans to earn her education certificate. In January 1995, she applied to a program in modern languages at Moray House, run by Heriot-Watt University in Edinburgh. She was one of 120 candidates for the thirty available spots in the program, which would begin in August. The application process included an intense daylong interview conducted in French, the language Rowling wanted to teach. She

Rowling earned her teaching degree at the Moray House in Edinburgh.

was thrilled to be accepted. It was a big accomplishment and a boost to her self-esteem. Rowling tackled her novel with even greater enthusiasm. By the end of the summer, she had completed a draft of the entire book.

During these months, she also received a grant from the Scottish Office of Education and Industry to help support her as a full-time student. This grant would help her pay for her schooling and textbooks. Rowling thought she was as ready as she could be to begin her studies. Then she learned that the university did not have a child care facility, as she had been told. It had closed two years before.

A friend who has never been publicly named miraculously came to her rescue, offering a loan of £4,000 ($6,400). "I broke down and cried when my friend offered it to me," Rowling later said. "At the time it was like a half a million pounds to me. It was this enormous sum of money. I think we both thought I would never be able to pay it back. The friend was saying in effect: 'Here is a gift to help you.'" The grant and the gift from her friend enabled Rowling to go off public assistance. She started working on her degree at the Moray House, which later became part of the University of Edinburgh.

Rowling posed for this photo shortly after her first Harry Potter book was published.

Chapter SIX

PUBLISHING
HARRY POTTER

ROWLING TINKERED WITH THE DRAFT OF HER BOOK, polishing it as time allowed over the next several months. Finally, in late 1995, the story of Harry Potter's first year at Hogwarts was finished. She typed the whole manuscript—all ninety thousand words of it— on a secondhand manual typewriter. Then, because she could not afford to make copies, she typed another complete manuscript.

Rowling's next challenge was to figure out who might be interested in publishing her story. At the library, she found a reference book that listed publishers, as well as literary agents. Literary agents represent authors and help them sell their work to publishers. As Rowling's eyes slid over the list of names, one agent in particular popped out—Christopher Little. She liked this name. It sounded like a character in a children's book. So she wrote it down along with a few others.

By this time, Rowling had spent nearly six years creating Harry Potter's world. She knew all the characters that lived there. She had plotted out each of her hero's seven years at Hogwarts. And she knew how Harry Potter's story would end. It was time to send Harry out into the world. With a mixture of excitement and apprehension, she started submitting the first three chapters of *Harry Potter and the Philosopher's Stone*, by Joanne Rowling, to the publishers and agents she had selected.

An Agent

At the Christopher Little Literary Agency in London, a young office manager named Bryony Evens was in charge of opening the mail. Every day, she sorted the manuscripts the agency received into piles—one to be rejected and another to give to her boss, Christopher Little, for consideration. When Rowling's three sample chapters arrived, Evens put them directly in the reject pile because the agency did not handle children's books. "But it had an interesting binder, with a peculiar fastening," Evens later recalled. "So I read the synopsis. It had all the elements of a classic." Then, as she read the three chapters, Evens found herself drawn into the story and was particularly struck by the humor in the writing. She asked Little if she could request the rest of the manuscript from Rowling. Based on her enthusiasm, he agreed.

When a letter from the Christopher Little Literary Agency arrived, Rowling was prepared for rejection. One publisher and one agent had already refused her, and she knew that the odds of getting a book published were not in her favor. Inside the envelope, however, was the two-sentence reply that would change her life: "Thank you. We would be pleased to receive the balance of your manuscript on an exclusive basis." Rowling was stunned. "It was the best letter of my life," she later said. "I read it eight times."

Rowling sent off the remaining chapters of the book immediately. And when the package arrived in London, Evens eagerly tore it open and started reading. "I had already decided that, even if we had rejected it, I was going to read the rest of it for my own curiosity," recalled Evens. "I remember making a mental list of what was great about it—it had the school story, it had the orphan living with evil step-family story, it had witches, wizards, and magic, which is always fantastic, and it was a really good detective story with a twist at the end." After making some notes, she handed the manuscript off to Little, who took it home and read it that evening. He returned to the office in the morning filled with enthusiasm for Rowling's book.

Little and Evens discussed the few improvements they would ask Rowling to make. Evens wanted

Neville Longbottom—Harry's friend and fellow Gryffindor—to play a larger role. And Little was quite taken with Quidditch. He thought the rules of the game should be explained. Rowling happily made the changes they suggested. She liked Neville quite a lot, so she did not mind increasing his presence in the story. And she already had the rules for Quidditch prepared. In fact, she had taken them out of her final draft, fearing that it was just too much detail. She even sent along a sketch of a Quidditch match.

When Bryony was satisfied with the manuscript, she showed it to Patrick Walsh, who was Christopher Little's business partner. He was impressed and agreed that the agency should offer their standard contract to Rowling. The agency would receive 15 percent of the book's earnings in the United Kingdom and 20 percent for foreign rights and film rights. Rowling signed on immediately. She had no expectations when it came to money. "I knew that most children's writers don't make any money. They will never ever, ever be very well known. I was totally OK with that. I just wanted someone to publish Harry so I could go to bookshops and see it," Rowling later said.

A Publisher at Last

While the Christopher Little Literary Agency worked on finding a publisher for her book, Rowling continued to pursue her education. The program grew more and more demanding as the school year progressed. By early 1996, Rowling was student teaching high school, and she faced tough evaluations of her classroom methods. Her initial grades were dismal, but as the year wore on, she improved and began earning praise for her professionalism, her ability to relate to students, and her carefully planned and imaginative lessons. She had a promising future as a classroom teacher.

Meanwhile, Bryony Evens continued to shop around *Harry Potter and the Philosopher's Stone* to potential publishers. Twelve publishers passed on the chance to purchase the rights. But thirteen would prove to be a lucky number. Evens sent the manuscript to Bloomsbury, a publisher that had recently started a children's book division. The head of the division, Barry Cunningham, was wild about Rowling's book. "It was just terribly exciting," he later said. "What struck me first was that the book came with a fully imagined world. There was a complete sense of Jo knowing the characters and what would happen to them."

Cunningham convinced the company's directors to support the book. They agreed to offer Rowling an advance of £1,500 ($2,250) for the rights (permission) to publish her book. The advance would be subtracted from Rowling's royalty earnings from the sale of the book. After deducting Little's commission, Rowling would receive a £1,275 ($1,910) advance. After the advance was paid, all royalty income from the sale of the book would go directly to the author, except for the agent's commission.

It was August 1996, and Rowling had just finished her education certification when Little called with the news. "I could not believe my ears," Rowling remembered. "'You mean it's going to be published?' I asked, rather stupidly. 'It's definitely going to be published?' After I had hung up, I screamed and jumped into the air." It was one of the best moments of her life.

Rowling holds a rare first edition of Harry Potter and the Philosopher's Stone.

IN THE BOOKSHOPS

While Bloomsbury edited her book for publication, Rowling started teaching. She took a part-time position at nearby Leith Academy, where she had done her student teaching that summer. The school had a child care center where she could leave Jessica while she taught. In between preparing lessons, she started writing her next book, *Harry Potter and the Chamber of Secrets*. Still shy about her budding writing career, she told only those closest to her about the upcoming publication of her first book.

Rowling's ambition was to be a full-time writer, a goal that seemed unattainable at that point. She and Jessica certainly could not live on her advance from Bloomsbury. And her part-time teaching salary was not enough to pay the bills. By chance, she heard about a writer's grant offered by the Scottish Arts Council. To be eligible, candidates needed to be a resident of Scotland and a recently published author. *Harry Potter and the Philosopher's Stone* had not yet been published, but because Rowling had a contract with Bloomsbury, the council agreed to consider her application. Based on the strength of her proposal and a sample of her work, Rowling became one of forty finalists for the ten grants to be awarded. The council's special panel granted Rowling its top award of £8,000 ($12,000) to support her while she wrote *Harry Potter and the Chamber of Secrets*. When Rowling received her check, she made a big purchase—a computer. Now, even though she still wrote in long-hand, she could abandon her old manual typewriter and use a word-processing program to type and revise her next book.

First published in Great Britain, Rowling's book (retitled Harry Potter and the Sorcerer's Stone *for the U.S. market) was soon in bookstores in the United States and all over the world.*

Rowling's first manuscript was so polished that it required very little editing by Bloomsbury. The biggest change Barry Cunningham wanted was in the author's name. Many boys, he had been told, avoided books written by women, no matter what the topic. He thought Rowling's book would be equally appealing to boys and girls. So, after much discussion, Joanne Rowling became J. K. Rowling. She gave herself the middle name Kathleen after her favorite grandmother. Later, when asked about the added initial, Rowling replied, "It was the publisher's idea. They could have called me Enid Snodgrass. I just wanted it [the book] published."

On June 26, 1997, J. K. Rowling's *Harry Potter and the Philosopher's Stone* landed in Britain's bookstores. Seven long years after Harry Potter wandered into her head during that train ride from Manchester to London, Rowling's lifelong dream had become reality. She was a published author. "I walked around all day with a finished copy tucked under my arm," Rowling later recalled. "The first time I saw it in a bookshop I had this mad desire to sign it. It was an extraordinary moment."

Harry Potter fans come in all ages from countries around the world. These two British fans have dressed up as Harry Potter.

Chapter **SEVEN**

POTTERMANIA

EVERY YEAR, PUBLISHERS FROM AROUND THE WORLD gather at the Bologna Children's Book Fair in Italy. Many search for foreign books to buy and publish in their own country. At the 1997 book fair, an editorial director named Arthur Levine from the U.S. publisher Scholastic picked up a story by the unknown British author J. K. Rowling. On the flight back to New York, Levine read *Harry Potter and the Philosopher's Stone.* He felt an immediate connection to the story and decided to go after the rights to publish it in the United States.

Three days after Rowling's book was published in Britain, the rights to publish a U.S. edition went up for auction in New York. Levine found himself in a bidding war. As the price climbed, Levine asked himself "Do you love it this much? Do you love it at $50,000? At $70,000?" In the end, he won the bidding, agreeing to pay $105,000 for the rights to publish Rowling's first book—the largest amount ever to be paid to a first-time children's author. It was also the largest sum that Levine had ever paid for a book. But he felt certain Rowling's book was worth the risk. "You have to follow your heart," Levine later said. "In Harry Potter, the wand chooses the wizard; and when the wand chooses you, you take it."

Levine's first thought after the auction was to call Rowling. He knew that a purchase price this high would put a lot of pressure on her, and he wanted to give her some reassurance. It was late in the evening when he reached her in Edinburgh. "The first words he said to me were: 'Don't panic,'" Rowling recalled. "He really knew what I was going through. I went to bed and couldn't sleep. On one level, I was obviously delighted, but most of me froze." She knew her life was about to change.

SUDDEN FAME

Overnight, J. K. Rowling became famous as the single mother who had risen from poverty to clinch an unheard of book deal. The press played up the Cinderella story, stretching the truth for dramatic effect. After all, Rowling had been on public assistance for only a brief time. And while she still struggled financially, she was not the newly divorced, penniless single mother the press made her out to be. But her rags-to-riches story intrigued people, and as they read about her in newspaper stories and interviews, sales of her book began to take off.

The sudden fame was unnerving for Rowling. She wanted attention focused on her book, not on herself. Amid all this hype, Rowling experienced her first serious bout of writer's block. She was having trouble finishing the next book, *Harry Potter and the Chamber of Secrets*. "I was worried that it wouldn't live up to readers' expectations—I'd heard that your second novel is the hardest to write," Rowling said. Two weeks after her first book was published, Rowling delivered the second manuscript to her publisher. She had met her deadline, but she was not pleased with her work. She convinced Bloomsbury to give the manuscript back to her and spent the next six weeks revising and polishing the story. Then Rowling set to work on the third book, *Harry Potter and the Prisoner of Azkaban*.

Throughout that summer, *Harry Potter and the Philosopher's Stone* moved up the best-seller list in Britain. Rowling's magical world and creative story appealed to children and adults alike, and book critics gave it high marks. In November 1997, *Harry Potter and the Philosopher's Stone* received the Smarties Prize for outstanding children's literature. The book won several more awards, including the British Book Awards Children's Book of the Year. Rowling's fame grew, and sales of her novel soared. A year after the publication of her first book, it had sold seventy thousand copies. And when *Harry Potter and the Chamber of Secrets* was released in Britain in July 1998, it immediately took the top spot on the best-seller list, pushing aside popular adult authors such as John Grisham and Tom Clancy.

Rowling dedicated *Harry Potter and the Chamber of Secrets* to her friend Sean Harris, calling him her "get-away driver and foul-weather friend." In one of the book's early scenes, three of the Weasley brothers help Harry escape a dreadful summer at the Dursleys. They pick him up in a flying Ford Anglia, the same type of

Harry Potter and his friend Ron have an adventure in the flying Ford Anglia seen here in the movie version of Harry Potter and the Chamber of Secrets.

car that Rowling and Harris used to escape their small-town life as teenagers.

The second book carries a theme of tolerance. Racist wizards in the magical world believe there is a hierarchy among wizards. They see pure-blooded wizards as the best. They call wizards who come from a mixed background of Muggles and wizards "mudbloods," which is a great insult. And they refer to those from wizarding families who lack magical powers as Squibs, a rude term. When Harry is faced with prejudice, it forces him to think about tolerance and base his actions on his beliefs.

HARRY IN AMERICA

While British readers were delving into the story of Harry Potter's second year at Hogwarts, U.S. audiences had yet to meet the boy wizard. In August 1998, Scholastic published Rowling's first book, which had been retitled *Harry Potter and the Sorcerer's Stone* for U.S. audiences. The enthusiasm of readers in the United States equaled that of readers in Britain. By the end of 1998, Scholastic had ordered seven printings totaling 190,000 copies—an astounding number for a children's book. *Harry Potter and the Sorcerer's Stone* was one of the year's top sellers.

When American readers learned that the second book in the series was available in Britain, they started ordering it from overseas. Worried about losing sales,

Scholastic began scrambling to publish *Harry Potter and the Chamber of Secrets*. The success of her book in the United States puzzled Rowling. She was surprised that American audiences would be interested in a story peppered with British references and set at a British boarding school—even if it was a school for wizards. But the location did not matter. It was the story—a tale of magic, friendship, and good over evil—that had captured readers' imaginations.

With the advance from Scholastic now stashed in her bank account and royalty checks slowly coming in, Rowling decided to make some changes in her life. She gave up her one-bedroom apartment and purchased a larger place in Edinburgh, on Hazelbank Terrace. There five-year-old Jessica would have her own bedroom for the first time. Hazelbank Terrace was a pleasant street in a friendly neighborhood closer to Di. Rowling also left her teaching job and became a full-time writer, a lifelong goal.

A year later, in July 1999, Scholastic at last released *Harry Potter and the Chamber of Secrets*. That same month, Bloomsbury released the third book, *Harry Potter and the Prisoner of Azkaban*, in Britain and sold more than sixty thousand copies in the first three days. Two months later, the third book hit the bookstores in the United States as well. By this time, the Harry Potter books were worldwide best-sellers. There were nearly thirty million copies in print, and the books were available in twenty-seven languages.

That summer, Rowling received her first £1 million ($1.5 million) royalty check.

Her third book was all that fans on both sides of the Atlantic had hoped for. With a darker mood and a more complex plot, *Harry Potter and the Prisoner of Azkaban* introduces Harry's godfather, Sirius Black, who has escaped from Azkaban Prison. Readers also meet Remus Lupin, a new Defense Against the Dark Arts teacher, who was a friend of Harry's parents. The Dementors, the guards of Azkaban Prison, also make an appearance. A kiss from a Dementor can erase happy memories and suck every last bit of joy and hope out of a human soul. In this book, a teenage Harry is becoming more self-confident and learning to fight evil. He also discovers that he must look hard for the truth and not always take what he sees and hears at face value.

FANS AND A FILM DEAL

Fans were eager to meet the author who had created Harry Potter, so Rowling started to attend book signings. "The thing I enjoy best—apart from writing the books—is meeting the fans," she said. "Answering their questions is pure pleasure." At these events, some fans bombarded Rowling with all kinds of questions, trying to figure out small details in her books or seeking clues to future Harry Potter books. Other young fans were simply frozen with excitement and awe at meeting their favorite author. One of Rowling's

Rowling frequently attends book signings. She likes meeting Harry Potter fans.

favorite encounters was with a girl she met right in Edinburgh. "When [the girl] reached the signing table she said 'I didn't want so many people to be here—this is MY book.' That really resonated with me, because that's how I feel about my own favorite books," said Rowling.

In October 1999, Rowling set off to the United States for a book tour. She was stunned to be met with crowds in the thousands at book signings. Long lines wound around corners. Some fans even camped out on the doorsteps of their local bookstores in order to be first in line to meet her. For the first time, Rowling realized the true impact of her work. She saw firsthand just how much people loved Harry Potter.

Hollywood also loved Harry Potter. Soon after the publication of *Harry Potter and the Sorcerer's Stone*, movie executives approached Rowling with offers for the film rights. She and her agent, Christopher Little, decided the timing was not right. They needed to establish the series first. Rowling knew the visual imagery in her book would translate well to the screen, but she had reservations. After all, she was still writing the series. It would be confusing if a movie added characters or took the storyline in different directions. She wanted a movie that would remain true to the book—and that included a British setting and British characters. At the end of 1999, the movie studio Warner Bros. agreed to meet these artistic requirements and struck a movie deal with Rowling for about one million dollars. As part of this deal, Rowling would have input into the script and some control over the toys, games, and other Harry Potter merchandise. Warner Bros. sold the rights to other companies to manufacture and sell toys and other Harry Potter-related items.

BREAKING RECORDS

Although there were great demands on Rowling's time, she tried to live a quiet, ordinary life. She took Jessica to school every morning and then hurried home to deal with fan mail, phone calls, and other business related to being a successful author. Still largely unrecognized in daily life, she could spend her afternoons writing in a café before returning home for tea and evenings with Jessica.

But this relaxed daily routine changed midway through writing her fourth novel, *Harry Potter and the Goblet of Fire*. It was the hardest book she had written so far, and she ran into trouble with her well-planned plot midway through. "The first three books, my plan never failed me. But I should have put that plot under a microscope. I wrote what I thought was half the book, and 'Ack!' Huge gaping hole in the middle of the plot." Rowling had to untwist her tightly woven plot and rewrite. Chapter nine frustrated her the most—she rewrote it thirteen times. Although Rowling worked for ten hours a day, she still missed her deadline by two months.

Harry Potter and the Goblet of Fire was finally set for release at midnight on July 8, 2000, in English-speaking countries, including Britain, the United States, and Canada. The book ends with an important plot twist, something that Rowling wanted to keep secret until the book was published. Books covered in brown paper were shipped to booksellers, who promised not to open or sell a book before the release date. Excitement for the book soon built to a frenzy, called Pottermania. Hundreds of thousands of readers preordered the book online, leading Scholastic to order 3.8 million copies for the United States—the largest first print run in history.

POTTER PROTESTS

The Harry Potter books might be worldwide best-sellers, but in the United States, they often top the list of books that people want banned from school libraries. Some Americans believe the books, with their spells and spirits, are filling young minds with ideas of witchcraft, the occult, and violence. Church groups that feel this way have held book burnings. Parents in California, Michigan, Minnesota, South Carolina, and other states have called for the removal of Rowling's books from their children's schools.

Rowling finds the idea that her books promote witchcraft and evil ridiculous. "Like a lot of classic children's literature, it deals with good and evil," Rowling said. "So my feeling is that their objection is utterly unfounded. I mean, occasionally, I wonder: Have they read the books? I think they're very moral books."

Many parents, teachers, and church leaders agree with her and have spoken out in support of the books. Educators and parents say they use the books to teach values such as loyalty, courage, honesty, and self-sacrifice. And many religious and academic scholars believe the books present moral messages that encourage children to do what is right.

Although there were a few leaks about *Harry Potter and the Goblet of Fire*, they did not spoil the book's release. In Britain Rowling set off on a four-day tour to promote the book. She stepped out of a Ford Anglia at King's Cross station in London to a crowd of five hundred cheering fans. From there she traveled

Rowling waves from the Hogwarts Express.

in a vintage train, christened the Hogwarts Express for the tour.

In the United States and Canada, lines of eager fans formed outside bookstores, waiting for the stroke of midnight. Some bookstores held contests, parties, and other special events. One store in Vancouver, Canada, threw a party that drew one thousand customers, half of whom had to be turned away due to overcrowding. A section of the Mall of America in Bloomington, Minnesota, became Potter Town. A store in Portland, Oregon, open for the midnight sale, offered 20 percent off for customers who showed up in their pajamas.

Readers immediately started turning the pages, soaking up Harry's latest adventure. In *Harry Potter and the Goblet of Fire*, a moodier Harry unexpectedly finds himself a fourth contestant in the Triwizard Tournament, a competition among three European wizarding schools. Harry must draw on his courage, wits, and skill to survive the competition. Rowling's story grows darker, more sinister, and more emotional with this book. And for the first time, there is a death.

Rowling's fifth book, Harry Potter and the Order of the Phoenix, *went on sale in the summer of 2003.*

Chapter **EIGHT**

LOOKING AHEAD

THE RESPONSE TO HARRY POTTER OVERWHELMED Rowling. With the record-breaking success of the fourth book, there were now seventy-six million copies of her books in print. She was fast becoming one of the wealthiest women in the world. Reporters were pounding on her door requesting interviews, and her picture was splashed on the covers of major news magazines, such as *Newsweek* in the United States and *Maclean's* in Canada. Awards were being heaped upon her books. Teachers and parents credited her with turning kids on to reading. Children who had never showed any interest in books suddenly could not wait to pick up *Harry Potter*. All of her readers were eager for the next installment.

Rowling felt immense pressure to begin her fifth book, but she was burned out. She could not face writing it. "The idea of going straight into another Harry Potter book filled me with dread and horror. And that was the first time I had ever felt like that," Rowling said. She did not want a deadline, and her publishers agreed to let her work at her own pace. She took a long break from Harry Potter, using most of that time to let the events of the past few years sink in. "I needed to stop and I needed to try to come to terms with what had happened to me," Rowling said. "For a long time people would say to me, 'What is it like to be famous?' and I would say, 'I am not famous.' Now this was patently untrue. It was the only way that I could cope with it, by being in so much denial that I was virtually blind at times."

Rowling had not completely abandoned the world of Harry Potter, however. She was involved in the upcoming film version of *Harry Potter and the Philosopher's Stone*, which would be released as *Harry Potter and the Sorcerer's Stone* in the United States. She worked with the screenwriter and sometimes visited the set to review scenes. Making sure the film accurately translated her book to the big screen was important to her. Rowling also wrote two humorous books, *Quidditch through the Ages*, by Kennilworthy Whisp, and *Fantastic Beasts and Where to Find Them*, by Newt Scamander. In the Harry Potter books, these are the titles of two books shelved in the library at Hogwarts. Rowling donated the proceeds from these books to Comic Relief. This group supports aid organizations in Britain, in Africa, and around the world.

LOVE AND CHARITY

Rowling was feeling lucky. She had Jessica. She had her writing. And she had financial security. Her growing wealth enabled her to buy a new home in Edinburgh, an ivy-covered mansion with tall stone walls to provide security and privacy. And because she was spending more time in London visiting with her agent and publisher, she also purchased a home there. Rowling was thankful for her good fortune. "I am fully aware, every single day, of how lucky I am," she said. "Lucky because I do not have to worry about my daughter's financial security any more; lucky because when what used to be Benefit Day [the day when public assistance checks are given out] comes around there's still food in the fridge and the bills are paid."

Busy with her work and her daughter, Rowling had pushed the idea of finding love to the back of her mind. Then one evening, while visiting a friend, she met a dark-haired doctor named Neil Murray. He had read ten pages of her first book during a late-night shift at the hospital. That was all he knew of Harry Potter. "And I thought that was fantastic," Rowling remembered. "He hadn't read the books. He didn't really have a very clear idea of who I was. It meant that we could get to know each other in quite a normal way." She found herself falling in love.

Rowling spent much of her time with Jessica and Neil. She wrote too, working on ideas other than Harry Potter, and she reserved time for charity work. Her newfound fame and wealth gave her the opportunity to help those causes she strongly believes in, particularly the Multiple Sclerosis Society of Scotland and the National Council for One Parent Families. She donated money, wrote newspaper articles, and made appearances in support of these organizations. A

In 2000 Rowling became an ambassador for the National Council for One Parent Families in the United Kingdom.

friend who had cancer inspired her to provide personal items for auction and hold book readings to raise funds for cancer centers in Scotland. Suddenly aware of her own influence, she began speaking out against injustices she saw in the world.

HARRY HITS THE BIG SCREEN

In November 2001, with Neil at her side, Rowling attended the world premiere of *Harry Potter and the Philosopher's Stone* in London. Set designers had transformed the front of the theater in Leicester Square into a copy of Hogwarts. Thousands of fans, many dressed as wizards, cheered the cast and other celebrities as they walked across the red carpet to enter the theater. Rowling was delighted to be part of the event, and the movie was all she had hoped for. Everything—from the characters to Hogwarts to Quidditch—were just as she had imagined them.

The actors—all British—made up what Rowling considered a "dream cast." More than anything, she had wanted Robbie Coltrane to play Hagrid and Maggie Smith to take the role of Professor McGonagall. Alan Rickman embraced the villainous character of Professor Snape, and Richard Harris became the wise headmaster, Professor Dumbledore. Rupert Grint and Emma Watson were perfectly cast as Ron and Hermione. And Rowling reserved especially high praise for Daniel Radcliffe, the young actor who played Harry Potter. "What Daniel's got, I

AN ART LOVER

J.K. Rowling has been an art lover all her life and enjoys touring galleries. When she was in her twenties, Rowling discovered a painting called *The Morning Walk* by Thomas Gainsborough that enchanted her. In this artwork from the late 1700s, a young, newly married couple takes a leisurely stroll. But Rowling's favorite painting is *Supper at Emmaus* by Caravaggio, which shows Jesus and his followers at a deeply emotional moment.

As a child, Rowling had great enthusiasm for art classes. Although she would not share her writing, she never minded showing off her drawings and paintings. Rowling still draws for pleasure. When she's working out in her mind how a character or magical object looks, she often makes small sketches.

Rowling also puts her artistic talents to use for charity. Her black-and-white pencil drawings appeared in her short works *Quidditch through the Ages* and *Fantastic Beasts and Where to Find Them*, which raised money for the aid organization Comic Relief. In 2004 Rowling wrote and illustrated a miniature book. About thirty pages long, this one-inch square book has a handwritten description of the items that Harry Potter needed to bring to Hogwarts. The pages feature illustrations of the objects, such as a witch's hat, a broomstick, and Harry's wire-rimmed eyeglasses. The minia-

Rowling's miniature book

ture book was auctioned off at a charity event and raised twenty thousand dollars to aid the homeless.

think, is the ability to listen and react very well on screen," Rowling commented. "Dan nailed it. And I am very pleased."

The movie earned mixed reviews. Many critics praised the special effects, set design, and acting. But nearly all agreed that by holding too true to the book, it lacked creativity as a film. And at two and a half hours, it was too long. Still, fans of the book were thrilled. The magical story they loved was unfolding before their eyes. It was magic at the box office too. The film set records for attendance the first weekend and by the following spring had brought in well over three million dollars.

THE *PHOENIX* RISES

While Rowling enjoyed living in Edinburgh, she wanted to find a retreat, a peaceful place away from the cameras and reporters where she could relax with friends and family. A few weeks after the film premiere, Rowling purchased Killiechassie, an estate built in 1865 on the River Tay in northern Scotland. Beautiful countryside surrounds the house, which is two miles away from the small rural town of Aberfeldy. It was at Killiechassie that Joanne Rowling and Neil Murray exchanged wedding vows on December 26, 2001.

Rowling had no time for a honeymoon, however. She was back to work on her next book, which would be titled *Harry Potter and the Order of the Phoenix*. She could no longer work in Edinburgh's cafés without

Rowling's retreat, Killiechassie, is in Scotland.

being recognized and approached. Instead, she set up an office at home where she would write all morning, take a break for lunch, and write more until Jessica came home from school. Then it was family time with Jessica and Neil.

This comfortable routine continued after Rowling announced in September 2002 that she was expecting her second child. She took time out in November to attend the premiere of the next film, *Harry Potter and the Chamber of Secrets*, another smash hit with fans. But Rowling returned to her writing immediately, eager to finish the fifth book before the baby arrived. "I was getting bigger and bigger and bigger and then, just before Christmas, I realized I had finished the book and it was the most amazing thing," Rowling remembered. "It actually really took me by surprise. I was writing the last chapter, rewriting bits of it, as you do, and then I wrote myself to the end of a paragraph and thought, oh my God, I've finished the book! I couldn't believe I'd done it!" Three months later, in

March 2003, Rowling's family celebrated the birth of David Gordon Rowling Murray.

Once again, the newest Harry Potter book was shrouded in secrecy. Retailers signed agreements not to sell the book until June 21, 2003. Pottermania reached a fever pitch. Prepared for the onslaught of fans, Scholastic ordered 8.5 million copies—the largest first printing in history. Then, at the stroke of midnight on the appointed day, thousands of fans around the world snatched up *Harry Potter and the Order of the Phoenix*. The book was Rowling's longest yet. The U.S. version weighed in at three pounds and 870 pages. Kids had waited three long years for this book, and they were ready to race through it. But some suffered the consequences, coming down with what one doctor dubbed a "Hogwarts headache." Some parents had to force their children to take breaks from reading.

Harry Potter and the Order of the Phoenix is Rowling's darkest book yet. Now fifteen years old, Harry is a moody and rebellious teenager, prone to angry outbursts. As he enters an intense year of study at Hogwarts, there is a growing rift in the wizarding world between those who believe the evil Voldemort is growing stronger and others who dismiss the notion as nonsense. Among the believers is Professor Dumbledore. Among the naysayers is the head of the wizarding government and his supporters, who try to discredit Dumbledore. They appoint the nasty

Dolores Umbridge as Defense Against the Dark Arts teacher and High Inquisitor of Hogwarts, and she sets out to make everyone's life miserable, especially Harry's. Once again, Harry must face evil head on, and once again, there is a death, a scene that pained Rowling to write.

BIG ANNOUNCEMENTS

By early 2004, Rowling could no longer answer her enormous piles of fan mail, so she set up a website—www.jkrowling.com—where she could relate news, dispel rumors, and offer tidbits about her books. In the first eight weeks, the website received 220 million visits from fans around the world.

In the summer of 2004, Rowling announced on her website that the title of her next book would be *Harry Potter and the Half-Blood Prince.* Fans immediately began speculating on the identity of the half-blood prince, but she would reveal only that he was neither Harry nor Voldemort. Rowling later announced on her website that she was expecting her third child, but she assured fans that her pregnancy would not delay the sixth book. The summer of 2004 also brought the film version of *Harry Potter and the Prisoner of Azkaban.* It won acclaim from critics, and Rowling declared it her favorite Harry Potter movie yet.

Over the next few months, Rowling posted big news on her website. On December 20, she told fans that she had sent her sixth manuscript to her publishers. A month later, Rowling gave birth to a baby girl. Mackenzie Jean Rowling Murray arrived on January 23, 2005. "She is ridiculously beautiful, though I suppose I might be biased," Rowling said on her website.

Harry Potter and the Half-Blood Prince hit bookstores in the United States, Canada, Britain, and Australia on July 16, 2005. The sixth Harry Potter book picks up where *Harry Potter and the Order of the Phoenix* leaves off, with a battle taking shape between the forces of good and evil in the wizarding world. Rowling continues to explore dark themes with her Harry Potter books, and death is once again a major part of the story. As events gather momentum and the final battle against evil looms, Harry and Dumbledore learn more about Voldemort's past in an attempt to under-

Fans in front of an advertisement for Harry Potter and the Half-Blood Prince

stand their enemy. Like its predecessors, the sixth Harry Potter book was a huge success with fans around the world. Later that year, the next film in the series, *Harry Potter and the Goblet of Fire*, was released. With worldwide box office sales of almost $900 million, the movie was an enormous hit.

THE FINAL ADVENTURE

On February 1, 2007, Rowling announced on her website that the final book, *Harry Potter and the Deathly Hallows*, would be released around the world on July 21, 2007. "I always knew that Harry's story would end with the seventh book, but saying goodbye has been just as hard as I always knew it would be," she wrote. Harry Potter has been with Rowling since he first wandered into her head in 1990. Since her first Harry Potter book was published in 1997, Rowling's books have sold more than 325 million copies in sixty-four languages. Four hit movies have wowed young and old audiences alike, and the film version of *Harry Potter and the Order of the Phoenix* is scheduled for release on July 13, 2007.

What is even more extraordinary is how Harry Potter has changed Rowling's life and the lives of her readers. From a bookish girl with a love of stories, then a teacher and single mother, Rowling has become one of the most famous and beloved authors in the world. She has inspired a generation of children to read and to tap into their own imaginations.

Rowling looks forward to continuing her career as a writer.

And she has shown how hard work, perseverance, and a little luck can lead to magical results.

Over the years, Rowling has changed only small details from the original plan for her story. It is still all about Harry. "He really is the whole story," she explained. "The whole plot is contained in Harry Potter: his past, present, and future—that is the story." Rowling has known the end of her tale for years. But she will not tell a soul. In fact, she wrote the final chapter years ago and tucked it away in a safe-deposit box. She refuses to say whether the ending will be happy for Harry and his friends. She has said, however, that the last word is *scar.*

Although the conclusion of the Harry Potter series is bittersweet for Rowling and her fans, readers can look forward to one more exciting adventure. "I'm almost scared to admit this," Rowling wrote on her website, "but one thing has stopped me collapsing in a puddle of misery on the floor. While each of the previous Potter books has strong claims on my affections, *Deathly Hallows* is my favorite, and that is the most wonderful way to finish the series." As for herself, she is happier than she has ever been, surrounded by a loving family, and able to focus on her life's ambition. Even though she will leave Harry Potter behind, she knows one thing for sure: "I'll be writing until I can't write anymore."

SOURCES

12 J. K. Rowling, *J. K. Rowling Official Site—Harry Potter and More*, http://www.jkrowling.com (July 2004).

14 J. K. Rowling, "First Person," *Scotsman.com*, April 22, 2001, http://www.entertainment.scotsman.com/headlines_specific .cfm?id=2109 (May 2005).

14 Lindsey Fraser, *Conversations with J. K. Rowling* (New York: Scholastic, 2000), 12.

14 J. K. Rowling, *The Not Especially Fascinating Life So Far of J. K. Rowling*, http://www.cliphoto.com/potter/rowling.htm (May 2005).

15 Rowling, *J. K. Rowling Official Site*.

15 Ibid.

15 Fraser, *Conversations*, 17.

16 Ibid., 24.

16 J. K. Rowling, "J. K. Rowling at the Edinburgh Book Festival," *J. K. Rowling Official Site—Harry Potter and More*, August 15, 2004, http://www.jkrowling.com (August 2004).

17 Fraser, *Conversations*, 15.

18 Rowling, *The Not Especially Fascinating Life So Far of J. K. Rowling*.

18 Fraser, *Conversations*, 13.

19 Rowling, *The Not Especially Fascinating Life So Far of J. K. Rowling*.

21 Fraser, *Conversations*, 23.

22 Ibid., 22.

23 Rowling, *The Not Especially Fascinating Life So Far of J. K. Rowling*.

23 Fraser, *Conversations*, 18.

23 Ibid., 19.

24 Ibid., 28.

25 Rowling, *J. K. Rowling Official Site*.

25 Fraser, *Conversations*, 29.

26 Rowling, *J. K. Rowling Official Site*.

26 Ibid.

30 Fraser, *Conversations*, 34.

30 Angela Levin, "The Penniless Mother behind Harry Potter,"
    Daily Mail (London), July 9, 1999, 13.
34 Rowling, *The Not Especially Fascinating Life So Far of J. K.
    Rowling.*
34 Ibid.
35 *Discovering the Real World of Harry Potter.* Produced by
    Questar, Inc. for American Public Television. Narrated by
    Hugh Laurie. Released on DVD 2002.
35 Rowling, *J. K. Rowling Official Site.*
36 Fraser, *Conversations,* 38.
37 J. K. Rowling, interview, transcript, *Barnesandnoble.com,*
    March 19, 1999, http://history.250x.com/vaults/c105.htm
    (July 2004).
38 Rowling, *J. K. Rowling Official Site.*
40 Ibid.
42 J. K. Rowling. "A Good Scare: The Wizard of Harry Potter
    Explains What Kids Need to Know of the Dark Side," *Time,*
    October 30, 2000, PAGE NUMBER.
43 Fraser, *Conversations,* 41.
44 Margaret Weir, "Of Magic and Single Motherhood,"
    Salon.com, March 31, 1999, http://www.*salon.com*/mwt/
    feature/1999/03/cov_31featureb.html (July 2004).
46 J. K. Rowling, Live Web Chat, *World Book Day Festival,*
    March 4, 2004, http://www.worldbookdayfestival
    .com2004/jkrowling_chat.html (July 2004).
46 Rowling, interview, transcript, *Barnesandnoble.com.*
50 Rowling, "First Person."
50 Rowling, *J. K. Rowling Official Site.*
51 Ibid.
52 Weir, "Of Magic and Single Motherhood."
54 Levin, "The Penniless Mother behind Harry Potter," 13.
55 Simon Hattenstone, "Harry, Jessie and Me," *Guardian,*
    (London), July 8, 2000, http://www.guardian.co.uk/weekend/
    story/0,,340821,00.html (July 2004).
58 Sean Smith, *J. K. Rowling: The Genius behind Harry Potter*
    (London: Arrow Books, 2002), 139.
58 Hattenstone, "Harry, Jessie and Me."

59   Ibid.
59   Philip Aldrick, "Lone Parents Are Poorer than OAPs, Says J.
     K. Rowling," *London Telegraph*, December 6, 2000,
     http://www.telegraph.co.uk/news/main.jhtml;sessionid
     =HH05R2UABC2OXQFIQMGSM5OAVCBQWJVC?xml=/
     news/2000/12/06/nrowl06.xml&secureRefresh=true&
     _requestid=101981 (July 2004).
60   Rowling, *J. K. Rowling Official Site*.
61   Ibid.
61   Levin, "The Penniless Mother behind Harry Potter," 13.
63   Tom Peterkin, "How £4,000 Loan Gave Rise to Harry Potter,"
     March 22, 2004, http://www.telegraph.co.uk/news/main
     .jhtml?xml=/news/2004/03/22/npott22.xml. (July 2004).
66   "Bryony Evens: Saved Harry Potter from the Reject Pile,"
     People, April 12, 2004.
67   Nigel Reynolds, "£100,000 Success Story for Penniless
     Mother," *London Telegraph*, July 7, 1997, http://www
     .telegraph.co.uk/portal/main.jhtml?_DARGS=/core/search2/
     portalAdvancedSearch.jhtml (July 2004).
67   Anjana Ahuja, "Harry Potter's Novel Encounter," *Times*
     (London), June 27, 2000, 2.
68   Roxanne Feldman, "The Truth about Harry." *School Library
     Journal*, September 1999, 136.
69   Smith, *Genius*, 159.
70   Rowling, *J. K. Rowling Official Site*.
73   Richard Savill, "Harry Potter and the Mystery of J. K.'s Lost
     Initial," *London Telegraph*, July 19, 2000, http://www
     .telegraph.co.uk/news/main.jhtml?xml=/news/2000/07/19/
     npot19.xml (July 2004).
73   Fraser, *Conversations*, 46.
76   Arthur A. Levine, "Why I Paid So Much." *The New York
     Times*, October 13, 1999.
76   Weir, "Of Magic and Single Motherhood."
77   Fraser, *Conversations*, 48.
81   Ibid., 53.
82   J. K. Rowling, interviewed by classrooms across America,
     transcript, *Scholastic.com*, October 16, 2000,
     http://www.scholastic.com/harrypotter/author/transcript2

.htm (July 2004).

84 Jeff Jensen, "'Fire' Storm." *Entertainment Weekly*, September 7, 2000, http://www.ew.com/ew/report/0,6115,85523_ 5l6999ll0_0_,00.html (July 2004).

85 J. K. Rowling, interviewed by Larry King, *Larry King Live*, Oct. 20, 2000, http://www.cnn.com/TRANSCRIPTS/0010/20/ lkl.00.html (July 2004).

90 Ann Treneman, "Hogwarts and All: The J. K. Rowling Interview," *Sunday Herald* (Glasgow), June 22, 2003, http://www.sundayherald.com/34715 (July 2004).

90 Ibid.

91 J. K. Rowling. "A Kind of Magic," *London Telegraph*, June 9, 2002, http://www.telegraph.co.uk/health/main.jhtml ;sessionid=YIHPFIIRPEGWJQFIQMFSM5OAVCBQ0JVC ?xml=/health/2002/06/10/fmrowl09.xml&secureRefresh =true&_requestid=35287 (July 2004).

92 Treneman, "Hogwarts and All: The J. K. Rowling Interview."

95 Andrew Alderson, "They Really Do Look as I'd Imagined They Would in My Head," *London Telegraph*, November 4, 2001, http://www.portal.telegraph.co.uk/news/main.jhtml? xml=/news/2001/11/04/npot04.xml (July 2004).

96 Treneman, "Hogwarts and All: The J.K. Rowling Interview."

99 Rowling, *J. K. Rowling Official Site*.

100 Ibid.

101 Ibid., *Larry King Live* interview.

102 Ibid., "J. K. Rowling at the Edinburgh Book Festival."

102 Ibid., *J. K. Rowling Official Site*.

SELECTED BIBLIOGRAPHY

BOOKS

Beahm, George. *Muggles and Magic: J. K. Rowling and the Harry Potter Phenomenon.* Charlottesville, VA: Hampton Roads Publishing Co., 2004.

Fraser, Lindsey. *Conversations with J. K. Rowling.* New York: Scholastic, 2000.

Schafer, Elizabeth D. *Exploring Harry Potter.* Osprey, FL: Beacham Publishing, 2000.

Smith, Sean. *J. K. Rowling: The Genius behind Harry Potter.* London: Arrow Books, 2002.

INTERNET SITES

"Harry Potter News, Rumors, Theories, Forums, and Fun"—*HPANA.* http://www.hpana.com (May 2005).

Rowling, J.K. Interview. Transcript. *Barnesandnoble.com,* HP Galleries. March 19,1999. http://history.250x.com/vaults/c105.htm (July 2004).

———. Interviewed by classrooms across America. Transcript. *Scholastic.com,* October 16, 2000. http://www.scholastic.com/harrypotter/author/transcript2.htm (July 2004).

———. *The Not Especially Fascinating Life So Far of J.K. Rowling.* http://www.cliphoto.com/potter/rowling.htm (July 2004).

MAGAZINES AND NEWS ARTICLES

Feldman, Roxanne. "The Truth about Harry." *School L ibrary Journal.* New York: September, 1999, 36.

Rowling, J. K. "First Person." *Scotsman.com,* April 22, 2001.

Treneman, Ann. "J. K. Rowling: The Interview." *The Times* (London). June 30, 2000.

Weir, Margaret. "Of Magic and Single Motherhood." *Salon.com.* March 31, 1999.

FURTHER READING AND WEBSITES

BOOKS

Colbert, David. *The Magical Worlds of Harry Potter: A Treasury of Myths, Legends, and Fascinating Facts*. New York: Berkley Books, 2002.

Fraser, Lindsey. *Conversations with J. K. Rowling*. New York: Scholastic, 2000.

Kronzck, Allan Zola, and Elizabeth Kronzck. *The Sorcerer's Companion: A Guide to the Magical World of Harry Potter*. New York: Broadway Books, 2001.

WEBSITES

J. K. Rowling Official Site—Harry Potter and More.
   http://www.jkrowling.com
   On this site, get Harry Potter updates, news, and the truth about rumors directly from author J. K. Rowling.

MuggleNet.com—The Ultimate Harry Potter Site.
   http://www.mugglenet.com
   Explore the Harry Potter books and movies and catch up on the latest news and rumors on this popular fan site.

BOOKS BY J. K. ROWLING

Harry Potter and the Sorcerer's Stone (U.S. title, 1998)
Harry Potter and the Chamber of Secrets (1999)
Harry Potter and the Prisoner of Azkaban (1999)
Harry Potter and the Goblet of Fire (2000)
Fantastic Beasts and Where to Find Them, by Newt Scamander (2001)
Quidditch Through the Ages, by Kennilworthy Whisp (2001)
Harry Potter and the Order of the Phoenix (2003)
Harry Potter and the Half-Blood Prince (2005)
Harry Potter and the Deathly Hallows (2007)

INDEX

OTHER TITLES FROM TWENTY-FIRST CENTURY AND BIOGRAPHY®:

Ariel Sharon
Arnold Schwarzenegger
Benito Mussolini
Benjamin Franklin
Bill Gates
Billy Graham
Carl Sagan
Che Guevera
Chief Crazy Horse
Colin Powell
Coretta Scott King
Daring Pirate Women
Edgar Allan Poe
Eleanor Roosevelt
Fidel Castro
Frank Gehry
George Lucas
George W. Bush
Gloria Estefan
Gwen Stefani
Hillary Rodham Clinton
Jack Kerouac
Jacques Cousteau
Jane Austen
J.K. Rowling
Joseph Stalin
Latin Sensations
Legends of Dracula
Legends of Santa Claus
Malcolm X

Mao Zedong
Mark Twain
Martha Stewart
Maya Angelou
Napoleon Bonaparte
Nelson Mandela
Osama bin Laden
Pope Benedict XVI
Pope John Paul II
Queen Cleopatra
Queen Elizabeth I
Queen Latifah
Rosie O'Donnell
Russell Simmons
Saddam Hussein
Shakira
Stephen Hawking
The Beatles
Thurgood Marshall
Tiger Woods
Tony Blair
V.I. Lenin
Vera Wang
Vladimir Putin
Wilma Rudolph
Winston Churchill
Women in Space
Women of the Wild West
Yasser Arafat

ABOUT THE AUTHOR

Colleen Sexton lives in Minnesota, where she has worked as an editor and writer for fifteen years. A graduate of the College of St. Benedict in St. Joseph, Minnesota, she specializes in nonfiction books for children.

PHOTO ACKNOWLEDGMENTS

The photographs in this book are used with the permission of: © ZBP/ZUMA Press, p. 2; © Getty Images, pp. 6, 99, 101; © Liam Dale Television, pp. 10, 17, 20, 29; © Hulton-Deutsch Collection/CORBIS, p. 27; © Gary Hansen/Independent Picture Service, p. 32; © Bryan Pickering; Eye Ubiquitous/CORBIS, p. 36; © ML001/ZUMA Press, p. 38; © Gareth Davies/Getty Images, p. 41; © age fotostock/SuperStock, pp. 48, 56; © Jon Arnold Images/Alamy, p. 52; The University of Edinburgh, p. 62; © AP Photo/Suzanne Mapes, p. 64; © AP Photo/Matthew Fearn, p. 70; © Jonathan Elderfield/Getty Images, p. 72; © AP Photo/Alastair Grant, p. 74; © Axel/ZUMA Press, p. 78; © Reuters/CORBIS, pp. 82, 88; © Joe Alvarez/Alpha/Globe Photos, Inc., p. 86; © UPPA/ZUMA Press, p. 92; © Toby Melville/Reuters/CORBIS, p. 94; © Randolph Caughie/Alpha/Globe Photos, Inc., p. 96.
Front and back cover: © Getty Images.